Durham *Quilts*

MILNER CRAFT SERIES

A Collection *of*

Durham Quilts

Muriel Martin

Printed in 2000 by
Sally Milner Publishing Pty Ltd
PO Box 2104
Bowral NSW 2576
AUSTRALIA

© Muriel Martin 2000

Design by Ken Gilroy
Editing by Lyneve Rappell
Photography by Sergio Santos

Special thanks to Carina Cox of Peppergreen in
Berrima for allowing us to photograph so many of
her wonderful 'bits and pieces'.

Printed in Hong Kong

*National Library of Australia
Cataloguing-in-Publication data:*

Martin, Muriel
Durham Quilts.

ISBN 1 86351 250 0

1. Quilting. 1. Title. (Series: Milner craft series).

746.46

I sit by the side of the broad rolling river

That sparkles along on its way to the sea;

But my thoughts fly again o'er the wide heaving main

To the home of my childhood so happy and free;

The sun with rare splendour may brighten each scene,

All nature in hues the most gorgeous may shine.

But all is in vain the fond wish to restrain,

I wish I were again on the banks of the Tyne

From *The Tyne Exiles Lament*
T. Allen
1862

ACKNOWLEDGMENTS

This book would never have happened without the love, friendship and support of my family and close friends. To my son Stuart (who was very brave and was my typist!) and his wife Angela, to my daughter Julia and her husband Flavio my deepest love and gratitude. I am a very lucky mother.

Special thanks also to my friends for their encouragement and help. Particular thanks must go to Tony and Nona Fisher; Paul, Amanda, Henry and Max Fisher; Susanna, Christopher, Charles and James Lott; Michael and Pauline Lyons and family; Gai Scott; Peter, Anne and Laura Cole and Paul Beudeker.

Sincere thanks to Nola Grabham and Leanne Fitzalan of Bathurst Fabrics and Trims for encouraging me to go further with my quilts and for supplying some of the 'extras' for photography. To Alison Snepp and the staff of Mosman Needlecraft for encouragement and advice. Also to Julie Ellis from Gumnut Yarns at Mudgee.

My appreciation to Libby Renney of Sally Milner Publishing, who convinced me that I could do this.

Most of all, my love to my Grandson Sam who thinks I am perfect.

**D**URHAM **Q**UILTING IS A CRAFT THAT WAS TRADITIONALLY PASSED ON AND LEARNED BY EXAMPLE. IT TAKES TIME TO ACHIEVE A CERTAIN DEGREE OF EXPERTISE AND PERFECTION. HANDS ARE NOT PRECISION MACHINES. THEY ARE GOD GIVEN. SOMETIMES THEY ARE VERY SKILLED BUT THEY ARE PART OF THE HUMAN BODY AND THERE IS A PLACE FOR A LITTLE IMPERFECTION.

STUDY THE CRAFT, READ ABOUT IT IF POSSIBLE, BUT DON'T TAKE EVERYTHING YOU READ AS GOSPEL. THERE IS NO PERFECTLY CORRECT METHOD. EVERYONE HAS THEIR OWN FAVOURITE OR SPECIAL WAY. THE METHOD THAT YOU ARE COMFORTABLE WITH IS PROBABLY THE BEST FOR YOU.

CONTENTS

INTRODUCTION

DURHAM **QUILTING,** or North Country quilting as it is also known, is an old craft – one that can be called, without offence, a working-class craft, and here I use incidence and examples from my own family history, and from memories of growing up in the mining village of Washington, County Durham (now in county Tyne & Wear).

My grandmother and great-grandmother where both quilters. My mother and aunts were fine embroiderers. I have a very clear recollection of playing under the quilting frame with the 'button box', which was a biscuit tin with a picture of King Edward 7th and Queen Alexandra on it. As I saw it, quilting was a part of life.

Quilting was also an escape from a harsh and mundane world, providing a little colour and luxury to an otherwise bleak life. In some cases it provided extra income for women. Women in my own family survived the deaths in mining accidents of my great-great-grandfather, great-grandfather and several great-uncles and cousins.

The mines were dirty and dank places. Men and boys spent up to 10 hour shifts of hard physical effort in dreadful conditions. Accidents and disasters were a fact of life. My grandfather told me of being sent to the mines as a boy of 12. His job was to pull back the leather 'doors', situated at intervals along the tunnels, to allow the pit ponies and their loads to pass. He told me that he would sit in the dark for hours listening to the noises.

For miners' families, home was a 'tied cottage' owned by the mine-owner. The cottage had a scullery, plus a room with a coal-fired range (in front of which my great-grandfather had his bath). Generally, there were two bedrooms. (Just imagine – my Grandma Maggie had 12 children!)

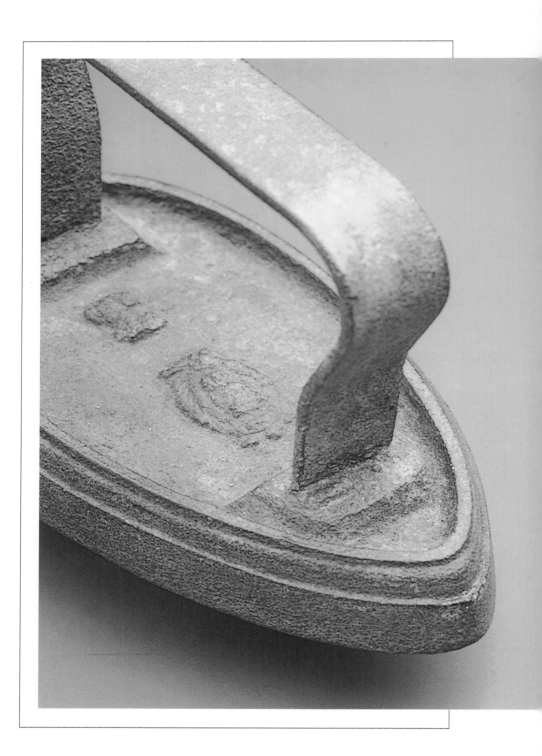

Some homes were lucky enough to have piped water in the scullery.

The houses were generally in what was called a 'row', like High Row, Coxon's Row and Brady Row. The toilet, usually an earth closet, was across the rear of the row, and known as 'the netty' (don't ask me why – I don't know!). Grandma Maggie's had whitewashed walls and a polished seat. She was very houseproud!

I learned by example how to make up the design for a quilt. There were no preliminary sketches or drawings. With some discussion, and perhaps a little disagreement, the quilt was on its way. This book comes out of what I was taught. I have adapted and simplified those experiences over the years, hopefully making things less rigid and easier to work, while still keeping to tradition.

As you begin to put together your own designs it is important to let the design 'flow'. Depending on the article to be quilted (and also on my mood at the time) I will mull over the templates for a considerable while before drawing up a maquette (model). Sometimes, though, I go in cold, drawing directly onto the fabric, and I must admit that this produces what is to me a most satisfying result.

Avoid using too many templates – particularly the 'itsy bitsy' ones – as the end result will be spotty. A very effective design can be obtained by using only two or three templates combined with $^1/_2$" (1.25 cm) crosshatching. The design will stand out with stunning simplicity.

If you wish to produce a traditional Durham quilt; play around with the templates, be patient, arrange and re-arrange until the results are pleasing to you.

13

Materials

Fabric

Good quality fabric is well worth the investment. Before purchasing the fabric, study the project carefully and think of its purpose. Is the quilt for you to use or is it a gift? Remember that a cot quilt will doubtless be well used and need frequent washing. A quilt made as a throw or decorator item will not require much laundering and will look elegant made in silk.

I suggest using good quality quilter's muslin, seeded homespun or polished cotton. I tend not to use calico because it's too stiff and course. Polished cotton gives a lovely effect, although the sheen will wear off over time. Dupion and Habutae silk give beautiful finishes, as does moiré taffeta. I suggest that poly-cotton, polyester or other fabric blends not be used if you are aiming for authenticity.

The projects in this book are either cream on cream or white on white, which makes them reversible. This is my personal choice. However, coloured fabric can be used if you wish. If you prefer to use a print fabric as backing I suggest a soft, delicate print. Please remember that the design will not stand out so well on a print fabric, so the quilt will not be truly reversible.

If you chose to use a design as a wall-hanging, a cotton print backing is acceptable. If you are confident of your quilting stitches, select a colour from the backing print and quilt your design in a thread of that colour.

If you are using quilter's muslin, wash and iron the fabric and remove the selvedges before use.

> **Hint:** I wash my muslin on a rainy day and hang it outside at the mercy of the elements it comes up soft and workable. It's best to then iron the fabric while it is slightly damp.
> If you are using silk, remove the selvedges but washing is optional (I do not wash the silk).

Batting

For a really authentic Durham-style quilt, cotton batting should be used (e.g. Cotton Classic or Mountain Mist®). Wool batting can also be used, and cotton/wool blends are also good. These are available from any good fabric shop. Polyester batting will not produce an authentic look. Never use iron-on batting as it will be nearly impossible to stitch.

Thread

- For traditional quilting using running stitch, I recommend Gütermann quilting thread or plain cotton. Use a colour which is no more than two shades darker than the fabric.
- On silk fabric use Gütermann silk thread.
- If you are working the design in chain stitch, I recommend hand-dyed silk yarns by Gumnut, variegated threads by Minnamurra and DMC embroidery threads. Use two strands of thread for chain stitch.

Scissors

- Good quality sewing scissors for cutting fabric.
- Embroidery scissors with sharp and tapering blades.
- Paper scissors. Apart from their obvious use, these should be used to cut or trim batting which has a tendency to blunt the scissor blades.

Pins

- Quilting pins (which are a bit longer than ordinary pins), otherwise use pins with coloured heads. Flat Flower Head pins are also useful.
- Small safety pins for basting

Pincushion

Use a favourite print and make one. Fill it with lavender for a pleasant effect.

Needles

I recommend sizes 9 to 12 depending on your level of expertise. The higher the number, the smaller and finer the needle. I prefer to use:

- John James Stainless Steel Quilting needles (size 11). This is a new size, which has the length of #12 and the diameter of #10.
- Piecemakers Betweens/Quilting needles (size 12).
- Bohin Embroidery needles (size 8 to 9) are good for working in chain stitch.

I suggest trying to avoid the gold coloured needles. They seem to have a coating that can be uncomfortable, especially for novice quilters.

Thimble

Use a thimble you are comfortable with. I prefer a leather 'finger' which looks like a cut off glove finger (to the second knuckle). This type of thimble softens with use and gives good protection.

Tracing Paper

I usually buy mine in sheets from newsagencies but you can also get it in packets.

19

Template Plastic

You can get this from any good quilting shop, but cardboard is quite acceptable. The back of cereal packs work well!

Markers

For marking the design onto the fabric I prefer a Quilter's Pencil by Birch or a General Insoluble Colour-Tex 1843 Silver. A soft lead pencil (H or HB) with a fine point is also good. Make sure that you mark with a light touch. The marks will fade out or come out with a gentle wash.

Quilting Hoop or Frame

Quilting hoops come in varying sizes. The quilts in this book are small; therefore they (and the cushions and table runner) can be quilted using a hoop or portable square lap frame. I suggest a 14" to 16" (35 cm – 40 cm) hoop or a 20" (51 cm) lap frame.

Sewing Basket

A wicker basket will hold all of your sewing essentials and can easily be carried around with you. Plus you will know where everything is!

Light table

One method of tracing the designs onto material is to use a light table. A light table can be made from an unused drawer. Have a light fitting installed inside and cover the top with a sheet of strong clear glass.

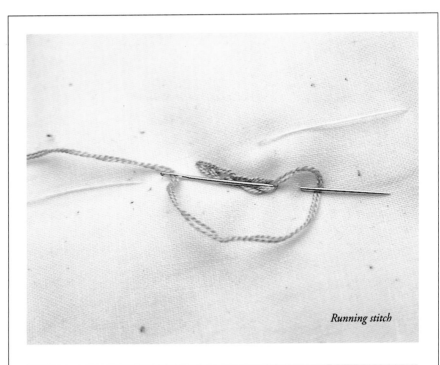

Running stitch

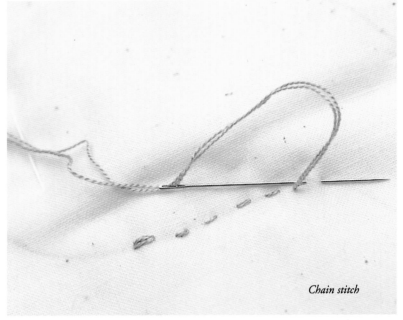

Chain stitch

Stitches

Running stitch

Aim to get three or four stitches onto the needle and try to ensure that your stitches go right through the backing. Your non-working hand (usually you left hand) will be underneath the hoop or frame. The first two fingers of that hand will feel where the needle exits. The stitching is worked with a 'rocking' motion.

It is most important that the stitches are even but no great emphasis should be placed on the number of stitches per inch. Stitch size is something that will evolve with practice and experience.

Chain stitch

Chain stitch

If the article being made is not intended to be reversible then chain stitch is an interesting stitch to try. It works well on cushions, wall-hangings, table runners and table covers. It can also be used on bassinette and cot quilts. If the reverse side is a print, then a colour thread can be chosen to match the print. Two strands of thread should be used for chain stitch. When worked carefully the reverse should resemble backstitch.

Designing a Quilt

The shapes used on the quilts in this book are, with the exception of three or four that were drawn up by my grandmother, fairly common and easily accessible. However by using these templates in a creative way, beautiful and original designs will emerge.

A close study of old quilts often shows that the designs are based on only a few (usually three or four) templates. If you are designing a quilt yourself, it is a good idea to use the 'less is more' theory. Take one or two templates and see how many patterns will evolve from simply repeating the shapes, in circles, squares and by reversing. Try to be original.

If you are gardener, walk around your garden; the leaves of geraniums, violets, ash and Japanese maple can make interesting patterns. Hibiscus flowers, lilies, water lilies and orchids have wonderful shapes and even architectural shapes can be made into designs. I generally carry a small pad of Ingres paper and jot down sketches of interesting shapes I see. Don't go into fine detail, just take the basic outline.

Choose a centre design that is in scale with the article that you have in mind. The centre design can be square, diamond, circular or even rectangular but it should never extend to the edges of the quilt. The centre motif will look especially effective if it is contained in a border.

Next, choose your corner designs. These should complement your centre motif and flow with the overall design and out to the sides.

You may like to repeat components of your centre or corner designs on the sides of your quilt, or you may like to choose a border design to edge the quilt. I prefer $^1/_2$" (1.25 cm) crosshatching but 1" (2.5 cm) is also acceptable. Experiment a bit and you'll find the effects are quite different.

Consider which type of stitching will go best with your project and whether you want to use a coloured thread or not. For a wall hanging, think of the wonderful selection of hand-dyed variegated threads available. For certain designs such as bed cushions or wall-hangings, these, used with beads, can produce a stunning effect.

Making Templates

Always make a master template from stiff card or plastic, and remember to write the name of the template on the back. It's a good idea to devise some kind of file system for your templates and to keep notes on their origins. There are three ways of enlarging the templates in this book:

1. By using grid paper. This is sold in sheets or in a book form and is available from most office supply stores or newsagents.
2. Using a photocopier. This is the easiest method but has its drawbacks. Photocopies—especially if greatly enlarged—are not always true to form. You will need to check the results carefully.
3. A pantograph, which is available from art stores and office supply stores. This will need patience and some practice.

Drawing up the Design

- I fiddle around with the templates until I'm happy with the result then I do a rough sketch on inexpensive paper usually draw up an overall design on a large sheet of inexpensive paper (like butcher's paper or cut-off newsprint paper).
- Then, if I'm happy with the look I put it onto tracing paper.

   On a sheet of white paper (tracing paper is best for this as it is quite firm), trace over the templates you have chosen. Outline these with a fine black marker.

- You may like to keep a small notebook with notes on the individual quilts, and what went into the design.

Marking the Quilt Top

The design is always drawn onto the right side of the fabric.

Cushion

There are three ways to draw up a cushion top. The basic method is:
- Mark the centre of the design with a dot or a small cross.
- Place the sheet of paper showing the complete design onto a firm flat surface. Keep it in place with sticky tape.
- Find the centre of the fabric by folding it in half by length and width. Finger-press the centre where the folds cross. Carefully place the fabric over the design, ensuring that the centre of the design and the centre of the fabric match up.
- Secure the fabric with sticky tape. The design should show through the fabric quite clearly.
- First, draw in the line around the design. Then draw a 1" (2.5 cm) border out from this, all around. Trace off the design, beginning from the centre and working outwards. Remember to mark the fabric lightly.

Another method, good for heavy or darker fabrics, is to use a light table. Tape the design and pattern onto the glass (with the light underneath) and proceed as above. Do not press too heavily on the glass. Accidents can happen!

You can also tape the design and the fabric onto a window and proceed as directed for method 1. Remember not to press too hard, and to work at a suitable level to avoid neck and shoulder cramps.

Quilt

- Place a white sheet (or a large piece of similar white fabric) over a firm flat surface. Smooth the sheet out and anchor it firmly to the table with adhesive tape.
- Take the centre motif of your design and place it in the middle of the table, ensuring that the centre is marked with a cross or dot.
- Find the centre of the quilt top by folding it in half by length and width. Lightly finger-press where the folds meet. Carefully place the fabric over the design making sure that the two centre markings match up.
- Tape the sides of the fabric to the sheet or table surface. Do not tape the corners.
- Measure a 1" (2.5 cm) border all around the edge of the fabric. Draw another 1" (2.5 cm) border in from that.
- Trace off the centre motif, taking care not to press too heavily. The markings should be lightly visible.
- Carefully insert the corner motif under one untapped corner of the quilt top, centring the motif into the angle. Trace off the motif and repeat the process on the remaining three corners.

FAMOUS NORTHUMBRIANS

George Stevenson: Railways

Sir Joseph Swan: Electric light

John Walker: Friction match

Captain James Cook: Born at Marton in Cleveland.

28

Crosshatching

One method is to mark the crosshatching lines onto the fabric using a long piece of flat timber (like a long ruler) cut to the required width (1" or $^1/_2$"). Another method is to omit marking the fabric until the design has been completely quilted, then commence the crosshatching using Quilter's Tape (or surgical tape like Micropore ® which doesn't leave a sticky residue). Lay the tape diagonally from corner to corner. Press the tape down lightly with your fingertips. Quilt along both sides of the tape. Remove the tape and carefully place along one line of stitching. Quilt along the unquilted side of the strip. Continue in this way until the quilt top has diagonal lines covering its surface. Repeat in the opposite direction until the top is fully quilted.

Using a Quilting Hoop or Lap Frame

First, baste the layers of fabric together as follows:
* Lay the backing fabric onto a firm flat surface. Tape it down to help keep it in place. Centre the batting over the backing.

> **Hint:** It is a good idea to spread the batting out over a spare bed or on a sheet on the floor for a couple of days to help it 'breathe' and fluff up a little.

* Place the marked quilt top over the batting and smooth it out carefully. Pin the three layers together all around the outside with safety pins.
* Baste the layers together, horizontally then vertically. Do not baste diagonally to the corners. This can distort the fabric. Use a neutral basting thread as coloured thread can rub off onto the fabric. When the basting is complete, remove the pins and any sticky tape that has been used.
* If you're using the lap frame pin the work into the frame so that it is quite taught but not rigid. You should be able to flick it with your fingers and it will bounce a bit.

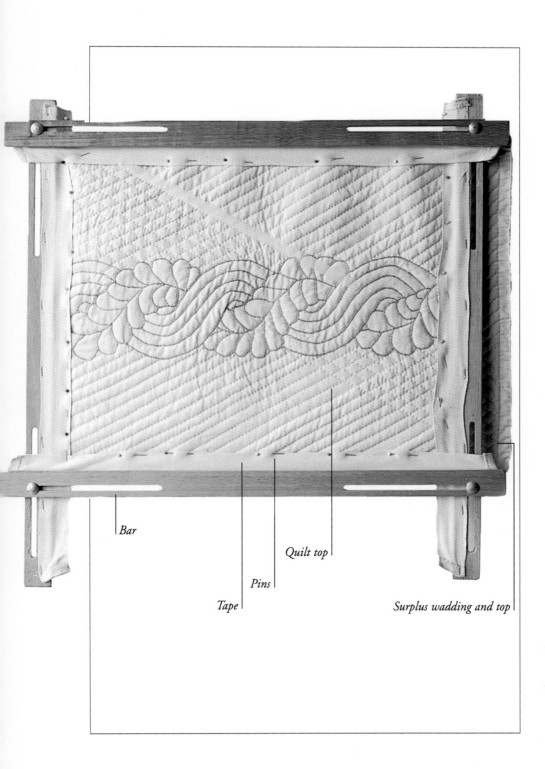

Bar

Quilt top

Pins

Tape

Surplus wadding and top

- When you are not quilting, a clean sheet can be placed over the work as protection against accidents such as cigarette ash, spills, small dingers and animals looking for a nice place to snooze!
- Place your work into the hoop when you begin to quilt. Remove your work from the hoop at the end of your quilting time.
- When you are not quilting roll up you work instead of folding it. The cardboard rolls used in fabric shops are ideal for storing quilts.

Quilting

The quilting process is done by using running stitch through the three layers; backing, batting and marked top. This holds the three layers together and produces the 'light and shade' textured effect that makes the design stand out.

It is best to begin with the centre motif, then do the corners, the sides and finally crosshatching. Begin stitching from the inside detail of a motif first. However, remember that with use and washing, the threads may pull so it is important to work the lines of the design as you would draw them not by stitching the nearest parts first. For instance on the Weardale Wheel complete the whole circle before beginning the 'spokes' rather than doing a piece of the circle then going down the line of a spoke. Also, don't run the thread through the batting between separate parts of the design. Over time the pull will show.

- Do not cut the length of thread off the reel before threading the needle. This helps to prevent the thread from unravelling. Thread the needle with a length of thread 18" (46 cm) long, then cut the thread diagonally.

> **Hint:** You may like to thread several needles at this stage to keep the process streamlined and efficient.

- Tie a small knot about 1" (2.5 cm) from the cut end. Insert the needle into a line of the design a short distance from where the quilting begins, going through the top layers of fabric and batting,

taking care not to pass the needle through the backing fabric. Bring the needle through to the start of the work and give the thread a gentle pull, bringing the knot through into the batting. Cut off any excess tail of thread that may be showing.

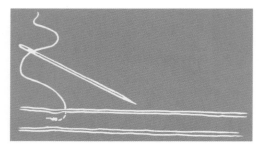

- Make a small backstitch then begin stitching evenly alone the design lines.
- Try to keep your stitches even. The ideal is an even length of stitch both front and back. Don't worry if your stitches are initially not very small – practice makes perfect! Very tiny stitches can produce a spot-like effect. It is also important to make sure that the needle goes right through the batting 'sandwich'.
- To finish off a length of thread, make sure that there is a reasonable amount of thread left in the needle. Make a last running stitch. Bring the needle from underneath and come into the middle of the last stitch to 'split' the thread. Make a small backstitch from where the needle emerges to the last needle hole. Run the needle a short distance between the backing and batting. Carefully clip off the thread.

Note: Try not to leave your needle in the work. If possible, finish off the length of thread you are using. Besides the possibility of leaving a mark, a quilting needle is small and could become lost in the batting.

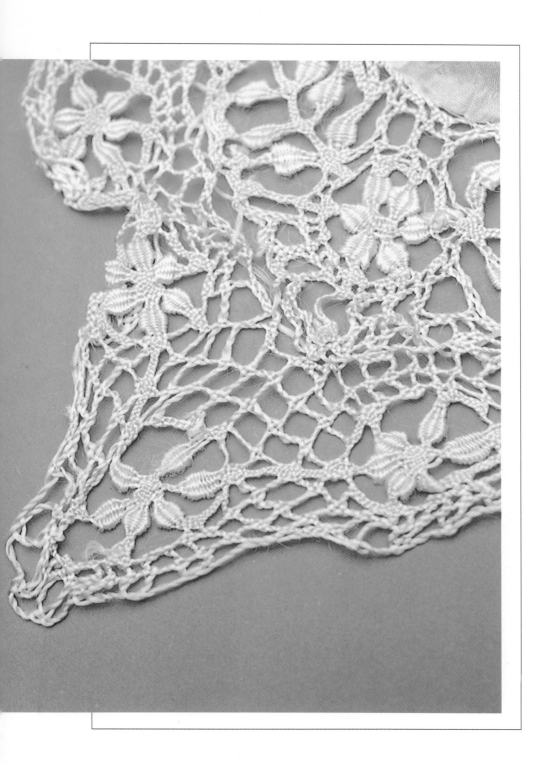

Finishing Off a Quilt

This method was often used on North Country quilts and gives a traditional look.

- Quilt the inner border using running stitch. The quilt design and crosshatching should not project beyond this border.
- Carefully trim the batting back $^1/_2$" (1.25 cm) without cutting the fabric. Fold the front and back fabrics in so that they are facing each other making sure that the edges touch the edge of the batting. Pin the fabrics together then tack them for ease of handling. Quilt a line of running stitches very close to the folded edge, taking care that the batting does not show through.

Finishing Off a Cushion

Make up the cushion to your own preference. You may choose an envelope flap, a zipper or buttons. Piping can be used around the edge but lace is never used for edging.

THE PROJECTS
Quilts

Lover's Knot & Flourish

The centre motif of this quilt is the Lover's Knot, a motif often found in North Country quilts and often used on quilts made for brides. This motif also appears at either end of the quilt.

Surrounding the centre motif is a wreath consisting of tulips and cowslip leaves, also referred to as Hairbrush.

Along the sides, and also forming the corners in a stylised tulip shape, is a design that appears to have no name, so I refer to it as Flourish. It is an elegant template, which lends itself to many possibilities.

41

THE LAMBTON WORM

During the time of the Crusades, one John Lambton, of a noble family, went fishing (on a Sunday – shock horror!) in the river Wear. The only thing that he caught was a strange looking worm, so he threw it into a nearby well. He forgot all about it, and eventually went off to fight the Crusades. However, while Sir John was away, the 'worm', which had grown to a tremendous size, emerged from the well. It terrorized the area, and when it had 'had its fill' wrapped itself, seven times, around a nearby hill.

The 4 $\frac{1}{2}$" (11.5 cm) wide border is Wineglass.

The crosshatching is $\frac{1}{2}$" (1.25 cm) wide.

The finished size is 42" x 55 $\frac{1}{2}$" (107 cm x 141 cm) and the quilt is reversible.

Materials

Fabric:	Quilter's muslin	88" x 58" (220 cm of 145 cm width), or 114" x 45" (290 cm of 115 cm width)
	Batting	44" x 60" (110 cm of 150 cm width)
Thread:	Quilting thread or cotton, one shade darker than the fabric	
Needles:	Quilting needles,	size 11 or 12

Fan & Wheel

After many attempts to draw this quilt design onto paper, I eventually resorted to designing directly onto the fabric. This meant that I drew the corners first, thus reversing the design process.

The centre motif of this quilt is made up of the template Weardale Wheel, which is 'echo-quilted' four times with $1/2$" (1.25 cm) between each row. This gives greater effect and emphasis. It is surrounded by eight small Banana templates, which are sometimes called Hammocks. These shapes also have two lines of quilting in their centre, again $1/2$" (1.25 cm) apart.

45

The template for Weardale came from a waterwheel at Killhope, in Weardale, where lead mining was active in the 19th century.

The Fan designs at the corners and around the edges are family templates.

The crosshatching is $^1/_2$" (1.25 cm) wide.

The finished size is 26" x 42" (67 cm x 107 cm) and the quilt is reversible.

Materials

Fabric:	Quilter's muslin	55" x 45" (140 cm of 115 cm width), or 44" x 58" (110 cm of 145 cm width)
	Batting	28" x 60" (70 cm of 150 cm width)
Thread:	Quilting thread or cotton, one shade darker than the fabric	
Needles:	Quilting needles,	size 11 or 12

CREST & FLAG

Northumbria's links with America. Hylton Castle, on the banks of the river Wear, near Washington. Displayed there is the Washington family crest carved in stone. Three stars and two stripes (Forerunner of the American Flag?)

Allendale Feather

A Rose, surrounded by eight Privet Leaves, forms the centre design for this quilt. The Rose template is widely known, but this actual template was drawn-up by my grandmother. I still have the wineglass that she used to form the shape. The corners are formed using the ornate Allendale Feather together with the simpler Rose & Feather.

The Allendale Feather is a beautiful flowing shape. Obviously, as the name suggests, its origins began in Allendale, Northumbria. This is a beautiful region, full of history. From Roman times the area had been searched for silver, zinc and lead. There are still forgotten

49

mine shafts in the area, which in its past has seen Roman Legions, Saxon, Vikings and Scottish raiders and Border Raiders. Pele (pronounced Peel) towers and 'keeps' can still be seen, these were fortifications used in English/Scottish border raids.

The crosshatching is 1" (2.5 cm) wide.

The finished size is 33 $\frac{1}{2}$" x 40" (85 cm x 102 cm) and the quilt is reversible.

Materials

Fabric:	Dupion silk	72" x 45" (180 cm of 115 cm width), or 72" x 58" (180 cm of 145 cm width)
	Batting	36" x 60" (90 cm of 150 cm width)
Thread:	Güterman white silk	
Needles:	Quilter's needles,	size 11 or 12

WASHINGTON OLD HALL

This is a restored old manor house. It was the home of the ancestors of George Washington. (The original Anglo-Saxon spelling is de Wessyngton)

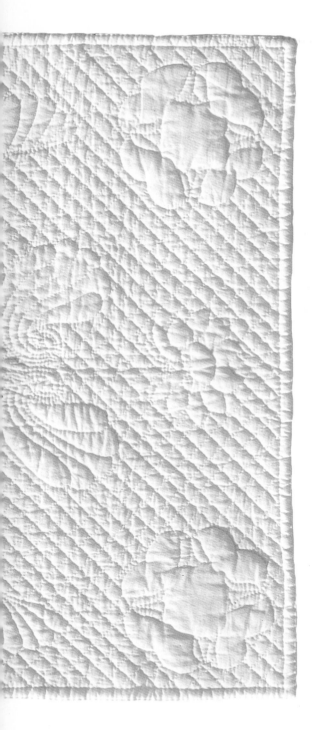

Blue Bell

My grandmother drew up the corner motif. As the flowers are bell shaped and my grandmother's name was Bell, I have named this template Blue Bell.

The centre motif on this quilt is the Lover's Knot within a $^1/_2$" (1.25 cm) border set on point (diamond shape). This border is framed within four miniature Goosewing motifs. Larger Goosewings appear at the sides, together with the Rose motif.

53

The Paisley Flower and Goosetail are used at either end.

The crosshatching is 1" (2.5 cm).

The finished size is 29" x 38 $\frac{1}{2}$" (74 cm x 98 cm) and the quilt is reversible.

Materials

Fabric:	Quilter's muslin	64" x 45" (160 cm of 115 cm width), or 64" x 58" (160 cm of 145 cm width)
	Batting	32" x 60" (80 cm of 150 cm width)
Thread:	Quilting thread or cotton, one shade darker than the fabric	
Needles:	Quilting needles,	size 11 or 12

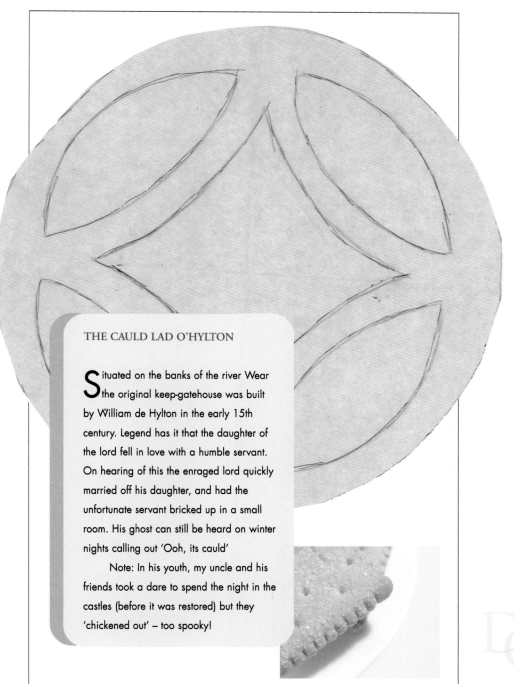

THE CAULD LAD O'HYLTON

Situated on the banks of the river Wear the original keep-gatehouse was built by William de Hylton in the early 15th century. Legend has it that the daughter of the lord fell in love with a humble servant. On hearing of this the enraged lord quickly married off his daughter, and had the unfortunate servant bricked up in a small room. His ghost can still be heard on winter nights calling out 'Ooh, its cauld'

Note: In his youth, my uncle and his friends took a dare to spend the night in the castles (before it was restored) but they 'chickened out' – too spooky!

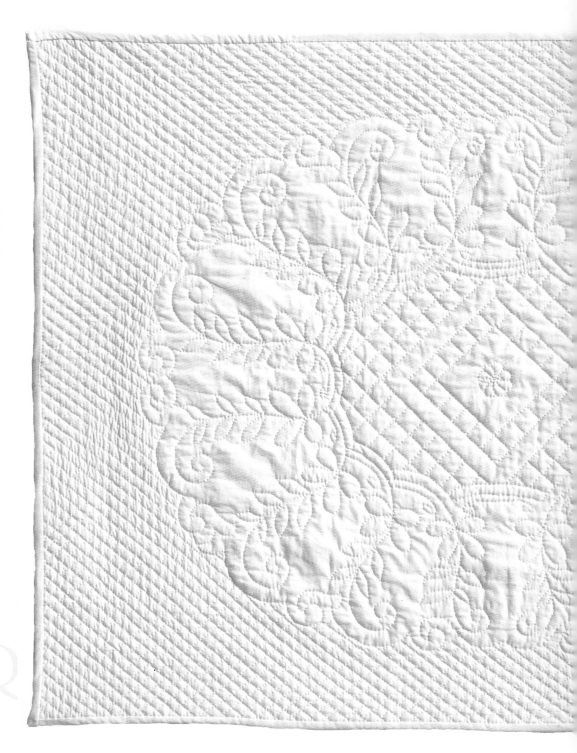

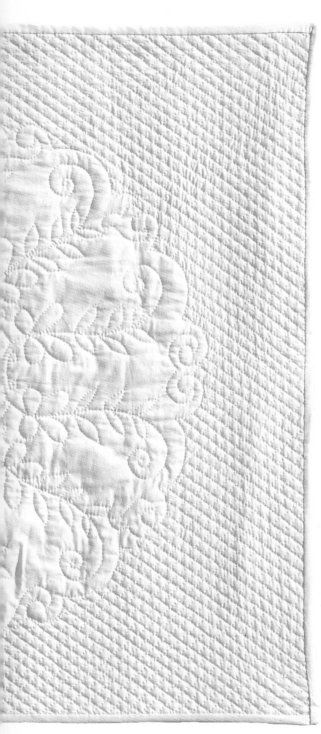

Leaves & Vines

This design, with its curves and leaves, has a style reminiscent of the 50s. It is quite simple but effective.

An initial can replace the Rose motif in the centre, or perhaps a flower or small spray of grub roses. If you choose to embroider an initial or flowers, do so before adding the backing, stitching only through the top fabric and the batting. This will mean that you will need to baste twice, but the effect is well worthwhile, especially if muted tones are used for the flower embroidery.

This quilt would be suitable as a throw or knee rug.

The crosshatching is 1" (1.25 cm) wide.

The finished size is 35" x 47" (90 cm x 121 cm) and the quilt is reversible.

Materials

Fabric:	Quilter's muslin	84" x 45" (250 cm of 115 cm width), or 64" x 58" (190 cm of 145 cm width)
	Batting	38" x 60" (95 cm of 150 cm width)
Thread:	Quilting thread or cotton, one shade darker than the fabric	
Needles:	Quilting needles,	size 11 or 12.

THE MINERS' MEMORIAL
(DURHAM CATHEDRAL)

Remember Before God
The Durham Miners who have given
Their lives in the pits of this County and
Those who work in darkness and danger
In those pits today.

Cushions

T his design has an old-fashioned feel about it. I have chosen to use chain stitch and embroidery thread but this design could also be done in running stitch with quilting thread. Whichever method you decide to work will be pleasing. The hand-dyed variegated threads produce a beautiful effect, particularly the softer shades.

There is no crosshatching.

The finished cushion is 18" x 18" (46 cm x 46 cm).

Materials

Fabric:
Quilted top and
cushion back:

	Quilter's muslin	20" x 45" (50 cm of 115 cm width)
	Backing (of quilting):	Quilter's muslin 18" x 18" (46 cm x 46 cm)
	Batting	18" x 18" (46 cm x 46 cm)
Thread:	Embroidery cotton or silk thread (two strands).	
Needles:	Crewel needles,	size 8 or 9.

ST. PETERS

St. Peters, situated at the mouth of the river Wear was chosen as a re-development site (late 50s/early 60s). The church would remain on the promontory overlooking the mouth of the river, but the graveyard was to be landscaped. During excavations to remove the graves, a mass grave was discovered. This was believed to be the result of a Viking raid because victims showed wounds made by axes, clubs etc.

THE PROJECTS

*Privet &
Welsh Tulip*

This design of Tulips and Privet Leaves is very simple and a good piece for beginners. It can be done in either chain stitching or running stitch. I have also made this cushion in silk, quilted in chain stitch and with a beaded centre, as a decorative bedroom cushion.

The crosshatching is 1" (2.5 cm). If quilted in chain stitch, the background has no crosshatching.

The finished size is 18" x 18" (46 cm x 46 cm).

Materials

Fabric:
Quilted top and
cushion back:

	Quilter's muslin	20" x 45" (50 cm of 115 cm width)
	Backing (of quilting):	Quilter's muslin 18" x 18" (46 cm x 46 cm)
	Batting	18" x 18" (46 cm x 46 cm)
Thread:	Quilting thread or cotton thread, one shade darker than the fabric.	
Needles:	Quilting needles,	size 11 or 12.

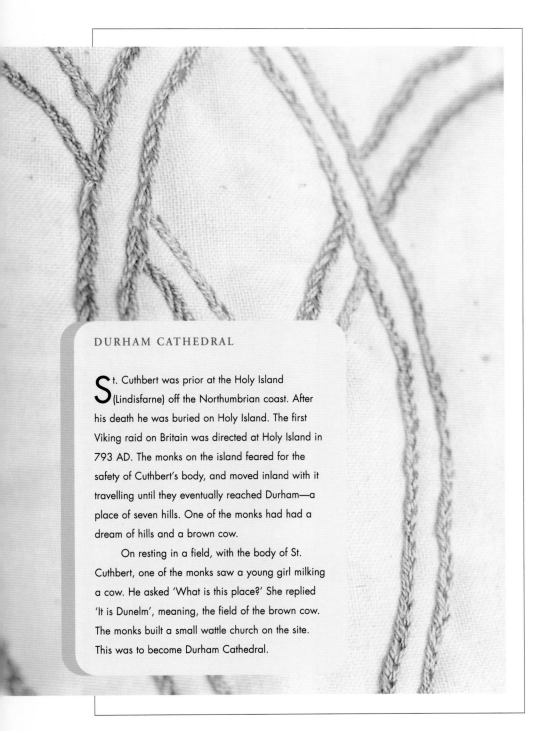

DURHAM CATHEDRAL

St. Cuthbert was prior at the Holy Island (Lindisfarne) off the Northumbrian coast. After his death he was buried on Holy Island. The first Viking raid on Britain was directed at Holy Island in 793 AD. The monks on the island feared for the safety of Cuthbert's body, and moved inland with it travelling until they eventually reached Durham—a place of seven hills. One of the monks had had a dream of hills and a brown cow.

On resting in a field, with the body of St. Cuthbert, one of the monks saw a young girl milking a cow. He asked 'What is this place?' She replied 'It is Dunelm', meaning, the field of the brown cow. The monks built a small wattle church on the site. This was to become Durham Cathedral.

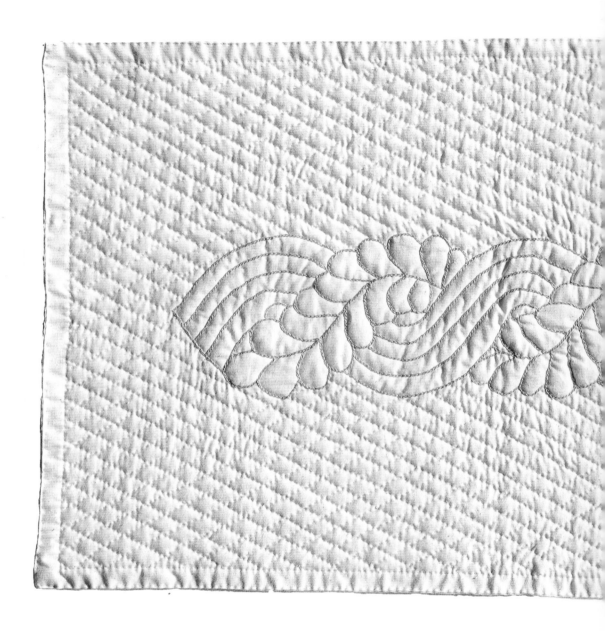

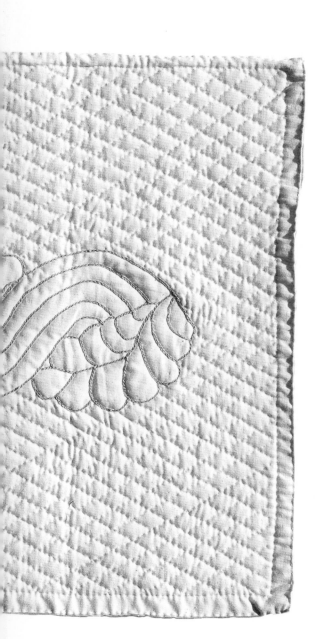

The pattern Rope & Feather is a simple but effective way of quilting this item.

This decorator accessory can be quilted in either running stitch or chain stitch. If you decide to use chain stitch, however, remember that the finished product will not be reversible. It can be given a festive air by backing with Christmas print (you will need 16" (40 cm) of plain fabric for the front and 16" (40 cm) of print for the reverse.) You may wish to pick out a colour from the print – green or red for the festive season – and choose a matching

69

coloured embroidery thread for chain-stitching the design.

The crosshatching is 1" (1.25 cm) wide and sewn in quilting thread one shade darker than the background.

The finished size is 14" x 42" (36 cm x 106 cm).

Materials

Fabric	Quilter's muslin	32" x 45" (80 cm of 115 cm width), or 32" x 58" (80 cm of 145 cm width)
	Batting	16" x 60" (40 cm of 150 cm width)
Thread:	Quilting thread or cotton thread for the crosshatching. Embroidery cotton for the centre design.	
Needles:	Quilting needles,	size 11 or 12
	Crewel embroidery needles,	size 8 or 9

JEREMIAH DIXON

At Cockfield was born a Quaker, Jeremiah Dixon, who, with his colleague Mason, was commissioned to survey the Mason-Dixon Line.

QUILTING ORGANISATIONS

New Zealand Quilting Association
PO Box 5664 Dunedin, Otago,
NEW ZEALAND

The Quilters' Guild
O.P 66, Dean Clough, Halifax,
West Yorkshire, HX3 5AX,
UNITED KINGDOM

National Patchwork
PO Box 300, Hethersett, Norwich,
Norfolk, NR9 3DB, UK

Irish Patchwork Society
PO Box 45, Blackrock, Co.
Dublin, IRELAND

Patchworkgruppe Wein
Grosse Mohrengasse, 27/14,
A-1020, Wien,
AUSTRIA

Belgische Quilters Vereniging
Dorpsstraat, 43, 3078,
Meerbeek, BELGIUM

Dansk Patchwork Forening
Peter Toftsvej 1, 6000 Kolding,
DENMARK

L'Association Francaise du
Patchwork
BP 40, 75261, Paris,
FRANCE

Patchwork-Gilde
Bundersweg 6a, 2000 Hamburg 52,
GERMANY

Quiltersguilde
Stationplein 38, 3818 LE Amersfoort,
THE NETHERLANDS

Norsk Quilte Forbundosstboks
195 Ulvoya 0139 Oslo 1,
NORWAY

Kviltforeningen Rikstacket
Renlavsgangen 28, 135 35 Tyreso,
SWEDEN

Patchquilt Postfach 55
CH-8024, Zurich,
SWITZERLAND

American Quilters' Society
PO Box 3290, Paducah, Kentucky
42002-3290, USA

National Quilting Association Inc.
PO Box 393, Ellicot City, Maryland
21043-0393 USA

Canadian Quilters' Association
PO Box 22010, Herongate Postal
Outlet, Ottawa, Ontario, KIV OC2,
CANADA